MW00975825

DIARY

OF A
MINECRAFT
WITHER

BOOKS KID

TABLE OF CONTENTS

Day 1 1

Day 2 4

Day 3 7

Day 4 8

Day 5 10

Day 6 13

Day 7 16

Day 8 19

Day 9 22

Day 10 25

Day 11 26

Day 12 30

Day 13 32

Day 14 34

Day 15 37

Day 16 40

Day 17 42

Day 18 44

Day 19 46

Day 20 47

Day 21 50

Day 22 52

Day 23 54

Day 24 57

Day 25 60

Day 26 62

Day 27 65

Day 28 68

Day 29 69

Day 30 73

Day 1

Mom sat me down today to have a talk. She said it was the talk. The most important talk I'd ever have in my life.

I was expecting her to tell me what scrambled dragon eggs taste like when cooked properly. I couldn't believe what she actually said.

"Willis," she began, a good start, since Willis is my name. "Willis, it's time I told you the truth about where you came from."

My heart sank. I'd suspected something like this would come one day. I'd always believed that I was born on the wrong side of the swamp. Our hut was in a lovely part of the swamp, with lots of boggy ground and dirty water to splash about in, but I'd always had a feeling that mom had found me on the other side of the swamp, you know, the part that edged the plains and led off into the great unknown.

"You see, Willis, you're not really a witch."

My jaw dropped. I'd always known that there was something different about me, but this was the last thing I was expecting to hear. "No." I shook my head. "That can't be true. I'm brilliant at mixing potions. You said it yourself. I'm the best witch at making potions you've ever met."

"You're right, you are the best at making potions. You have a natural flair for it. That part was true. But you're still not a witch."

"What am I?"

"You're a wither, Willis."

"A wither?!" I couldn't believe my ears. "No, you're wrong. There must be some mistake. I can't possibly be a wither."

Mom took me by the hand and led me over to the nearest still water. "Look at yourself."

I peered into the water. Three heads stared back up at me.

"Didn't you ever wonder why you looked so different from me? Why the hut is so much bigger than all the other witch huts so you can fit into it?"

"I don't know, mom." I shrugged. "I always thought my extra heads were maybe the result of a spell gone wrong. I always thought that one day you'd fix it, although to be honest, I like being able to see in three directions at once."

"Oh, Willis. You always were such a sweet boy." Mom hugged me. "No, as much as it pains me to say it, you have three heads because that's the way you were made. I created you one dark and stormy night in an experiment to see if I could make the perfect witch's familiar, and you have been very helpful to me over the years, but I think the time has come to let you go off into the world and find your own way. You need to find other withers to be with. You don't want to stay in the swamp with an old witch like me."

"I do, mom!" I protested. "I love being here with you."

"Well, if you really want to stay, you can, but I want you to know that you're free to leave and be with your own kind any time you like."

"Thanks, mom. You're the best."

Day 2

"Tell me more about how you created me, mom." I curled up at the bottom of mom's bed as she moved around, mixing ingredients together to make some splash potions.

"It was a dark and stormy night," she replied. "I'd just fought a Minecraftian who thought he could help himself to the contents of my potion cupboard. Instead, it was me who got to help myself to the contents of his backpack. Most of it wasn't very useful, although there was a rather delicious pumpkin pie I enjoyed for dinner, but when I discovered three wither skeleton skulls at the bottom of his bag, I had an idea."

"You made me!"

"I did indeed," she nodded. "I'd been feeling rather lonely and I wanted someone to help me make my potions. I'd been considering setting up a potion selling business, maybe even moving out of the swamp and retiring to a village where there would be plenty of passing Minecraftians wanting to buy my wares." She cackled. "Of course, that was never really going to happen. I'd be far too tempted to destroy the village, but the wither skeleton skulls gave me the opportunity to have some company. No witch had ever used a wither for a familiar and I wanted to know if it could be done."

A faraway look came over her face as she thought about that time so long ago.

"I put together some soul sand in a T shape before placing the wither skeleton skulls in just the right place. There was a loud boom of thunder and a flash of lightning. My creation – you – was alive!"

My skin tingled. Mom had never talked about this before. It sounded so exciting!

"You flashed blue, growing in size and strength before my very eyes. I stepped back, wondering if I'd gone too far. Withers are very powerful and you could have destroyed me without even thinking about it."

"I would never hurt you, mom," I told her loyally.

"I know that now, but at the time, I'll admit to feeling more than a little frightened. I even considered undoing the spell that had made you, but it was too late. As you grew, power oozed from every part of your being and I knew that if I tried to attack you, I'd lose the fight. All I could do was step back and watch you grow and hope that I hadn't gone too far."

I tried to imagine what it must have been like for her. It's true that I am very big for my age, but I always thought that that was just because I always ate all of my dinners, even the bits I didn't like.

"At last, there was a huge explosion. I ducked down, curling into a ball and covering my ears to protect them from the strange sound that played. It felt as though it could be heard through all of Minecraftia."

"I think I remember that sound," I told her, although I didn't. I'd forgotten everything about my creation.

"Once the dust had settled, I looked up to see that the explosion had completely leveled my hut. 'Look what you've done!' I screeched, forgetting for a moment that I was facing one of the most powerful creatures in Minecraftia. 'You've destroyed my home!' 'I'm sorry, mistress,' you replied. 'How can I make amends?' 'You can start by calling me… mom.'"

She looked over at me, smiling affectionately. "And that's how you came to be my adopted wither son."

Day 3

I know that I'd told mom that I wanted to stay with her, but now that I know that I'm a wither, I feel more and more like I want to go out and find other withers and do wither things and eat wither food.

I wouldn't know where to start looking though. I always thought that I belonged in the swamp, but I've never seen another wither here, so I guess I have to go out into the big wide world and see if I can find more of my kind.

It's scary thinking about leaving the swamp, though. It's the only home I've ever known. Sometimes mom went out to the plains, taking me with her while she's gathered ingredients for a potion, but that's as far as I've ever gone.

How will I cope without her to make my meals?

Day 4

"Mom…" I spoke hesitantly, not sure how happy she would be when she heard what I was about to say.

"Yes, Willis? What is it? Come on, boy. Spit it out!"

"Did you really mean it when you said that it was OK for me to go and find other withers?"

Mom put down her potion making equipment and turned to face me. "Is this why you've been like a bear with a sore head for the past couple of days?"

I nodded.

"I could tell there was something on your mind. Why didn't you say something sooner? Of course it's fine for you to go and find other withers. Didn't I tell you that I wanted you to do that?"

"Well, yes, but I wasn't sure if you really meant it. Maybe you were just saying it but hoping I'd stay here."

"Of course I'd like you to stay. I don't want you to think that you're not welcome here anymore. You can stay here for as long as you like, and if one day you decide to come back here with your wither friends, I'd love to see you again. But I've always known that there was a part of you that felt you didn't belong here, and you need to be with other withers now. Go on. Go find some friends and be happy. You deserve it."

"Thanks, mom. You're the best!" I hugged her tightly. "Now could you help me pack some food to take...?"

Day 5

"Now then, Willis. I've packed enough food to keep you going for a week, but after that you're on your own, understand?"

"Yes, mom."

"Remember – you're a wither. You shouldn't have any problems getting anything you want. If you can't get anyone to sell you food, just take it. In fact, don't even bother trying to buy anything. Take whatever you want and don't let anyone tell you that you can't. Withers don't have to pay for anything when you're as powerful as you are."

"Take whatever I want. Got it."

I nodded as mom continued to give me instructions on how to survive in Minecraftia now that I was leaving to go and find more of my kind. It was hard to believe that this day was finally here. I was going to find out what lay beyond the swamp and find other withers just like me.

"I've put a map in your bag as well, to help you plan where you should go. You can find withers all over Minecraftia if you know where to look."

"Have you marked those places for me, then?"

Mom looked sheepish. "I don't know where to look," she admitted. "But maybe you could mark the places on the map. I figured you could at least decide on the places that looked interesting to visit when you plotted out your route."

"OK, mom." I started pondering where I might like to go. Perhaps I should visit the desert, get some sunshine. The swamp was my home, but it was always so damp and miserable. The idea of some sunbathing was very appealing.

"Send me a postcard from all the places you visit, you hear?" Mom's eyes were misty and I had to admit that I was feeling like I wanted to cry as well. "I want to know all about your adventures. I'm going to worry about you, so make sure you let me know that you're safe."

"I will, mom," I promised.

"OK. Now give me a hug and then scram, will you? You've spent enough time dithering about. Time for you to go out and explore the world!"

Mom hugged me so tightly, I could barely breathe. "Mom... you're... squishing... me..." I gasped. She barely loosened her grip.

Just when I thought I was going to black out, she let go of me, pushing me away from her. "Go on!" she ordered. "Get out of here!"

I grinned at her, knowing that she was being harsh to cover up how upset she was. Waving goodbye, I picked up my bag and left the only home I'd ever known.

Day 6

The plains go on forever! I had no idea that Minecraftia was so big!

There are a lot of horses living on the plains, but every time I try to get near one, they run away. It's such a shame. I've always wanted to ride a horse.

I've spent all day slithering across the plains, but nothing changes. I certainly haven't seen any signs of other withers. Maybe mom was wrong. Maybe there aren't any other withers. After all, she said that she made me using magic. Maybe I'm a one of a kind!

Once I'd had the idea that I might be the only wither in the world, I couldn't stop thinking about it. If I was right, then it was pointless going off on an adventure like this. I could stay home with mom and help her build a potion making business.

I turned round. I could still just about make out the edge of the swamp on the horizon. It wasn't too late to go back.

"Aaarggh! A wither!"

I heard the cry in the distance. I spun round to see who had screamed, but I couldn't see anyone. I figured that they had run away as soon as they saw me so that I wouldn't chase after them.

Well, that answered one question. If I was the only wither, then nobody would have heard of me to know that they should be afraid of me.

But why were people so scared of withers? It was a mystery to me.

I frowned as I tried to puzzle it through. Suddenly, something shot out from me, exploding when it hit the ground a way away.

What was that?

I raced towards it. There, in the middle of the blast zone was something that looked uncannily like one of my heads. In fact, it looked so much like one of my heads that I had to pat all three to make sure that they were all still attached to my body!

Phew. All three were still firmly attached. But that didn't explain what had just happened.

I wonder… I wonder…

As I was thinking about it, BAM! It happened again! A wither skull went shooting off in the distance, making a loud explosion when it hit the ground.

I could shoot out bombs just by thinking about it! Awesome!

I had to practice this new skill. Why didn't I realize I could do this before?

I spent all afternoon floating around the plains, seeing if I could control where the skulls went. It took a lot of practice, but by the time the sun went down, I was able to set off a skull whenever I wanted in whatever direction I liked. I was really good too, hitting my target every time. Well, almost every time.

That poor horse.

Day 7

As I went over the top of a hill, I gasped when I saw what was waiting in the valley below. A village! Full of Minecraftians! I was sure that they'd be able to tell me where I could find other withers. At the rate I was going, I could spend the rest of my life wandering around Minecraftia and never see another one like me. Perhaps I could find a guide who'd be happy to travel with me.

The thought of having some company after a few days all by myself was enough to send me speeding down the hill. Maybe there were other witches there!

I couldn't remember when I'd last been this excited.

I suppose it was my fault that it all went wrong. I should have practiced controlling my new found skull throwing skill instead of just accuracy before I tried to go into polite company.

As I rushed down the hill towards the village, I sent a skull hurtling into the heart of the town.

BOOM!

Buildings exploded, villagers went flying and iron golems came rushing out to fight. I'd never seen anything like it.

I tried to explain that it had been an accident, but nobody wanted to listen to me.

POW!

Suddenly, an arrow was stuck in my shoulder. An actual arrow! They were shooting at me!

A red rage came over me and I'm ashamed to say that I wasn't thinking straight. I sent a skull right back, blowing up even more of the village. The iron golems were tough, though, and they started hitting me.

It really hurt.

As my health went down, I could feel my skin toughening and arrows began to bounce off me.

Ha! See how you like that, villagers!

Still, it was becoming very clear that I was outnumbered and if I continued to fight, I was going to lose, so I put all my effort into throwing a highly explosive skull into the troops attacking me and while they were distracted, rushing off as quickly as I can. I didn't care where I ran to. All I wanted to do was get away.

Some of the villagers and golems chased after me for a while, but I was too fast and at last, I'd left them all behind me. I could see some trees up ahead, so I went into the forest. I found a safe place to hide and curled up, falling asleep almost as soon as I closed my eyes.

Day 8

"Mom? Is that you?" My eyes fluttered open to see a witch leaning over me.

"I'd be amazed if I was your mother!" she cackled.

I sat up, wiping the sleep from my eyes. Now that I could get a closer look, I could see that she didn't really look anything like my mom. Her nose was slightly bigger and pointier, her eyes closer together and her robe wasn't nearly as nice.

"I'm sorry, mistress witch. Please forgive me for the misunderstanding."

"Mistress witch? Now I've heard it all!" She laughed again, a cruel laugh that I didn't find funny at all.

"I'm sorry," I apologized again. "Maybe you'd prefer it if I called you Hook Nose."

That wiped the smile off her face.

"That's more like it. I'd expect nothing less than rudeness from a wither. It's been a while since I've seen one of your kind round here. What brings you to my forest?"

"Rude withers? You mean you've met other creatures like me?"

"Of course I have. My goodness, you really are the strangest wither I've ever met. You have no idea how you're supposed to behave, do you?"

"I was raised by a witch," I told her.

"Ah. That explains it." She eyed me appraisingly. "Well, respect to whoever it was that created you. There aren't many witches brave enough to take on a wither. You things are powerful."

"I'm beginning to realize that," I said. "I just blew up half a village by accident."

"The village in the valley?" She threw her head back and roared with laughter. "Serves them right, the snooty lot. Did you know that they always send their iron golems out to attack me whenever I dare to leave this forest? Just because there was that one time I led an army of zombies out to attack them. You can't blame a witch for trying. You'd think they'd let bygones be bygones."

It was my turn to look at the witch. She seemed a deeply unpleasant person, nothing at all like my lovely mom. At the same time, she claimed to have met withers before, so she could be useful to me.

"Could you tell me where I can find some other withers?" I asked her.

"Of course I could, my little friend."

"The name's Willis."

"Willis, you say? Well, my name's Mabel. Come back to my hut and let's talk."

Day 9

Mabel's hut looks just like mom's hut, but it isn't nearly as nice. For starters, it has Mabel living in it instead of mom, and Mabel doesn't seem to like housework very much. OK, mom has always had me to help keep the place tidy, but that's still no excuse for letting your mushrooms go bad.

"It's so good to have someone else here," Mabel said as she bustled about, putting together ingredients for a potion. "I've always wanted someone to help me out. Villagers are so biased against witches. Just because there was that one time I threw a heap of potions of harming at the village. You'd think I was nothing but trouble, the way they treat me!"

I didn't say anything. It was becoming increasingly clear that Mabel was more than just trouble. She was a real pain. I didn't think she would be able to help me find any other withers at all.

"I'm sorry to hear that, Mabel," I replied politely. "And thank you so much for letting me stay here overnight. Your bed is very comfortable."

It wasn't comfortable at all. It was full of lumps, and I couldn't sleep for the sound of Mabel's snoring as she curled up in a chair.

"You are very welcome, Willis. I've loved having you stay. I was hoping that you'd want to stay a bit longer. A witch trained wither would be very useful around this place. I'd pay you with slugs and snails."

"That's very kind of you," I replied, even though inwardly I was cringing. What would I want with slugs and snails? Did she think that that's what withers eat or something? "But I'm on a mission to find other withers and I can't stay. Maybe when I've found some other withers I can come back and work for you." Maybe never I added in my head.

"I understand." Mabel looked sad, but thoughtful, as she nodded. "Come on then. Let me show you the best way to go to find other withers. There were some near here not very long ago. If you're fast, you might be able to catch them."

"Really? That would be terribly kind of you!"

Perhaps Mabel wasn't so bad after all.

"After you." She indicated for me to go through the door and I stepped out into the sunshine.

SPLASH! I was hit in the back by something. Something that shattered and dripped down. I tried to move, but it felt as though I was moving through water, all my movements slow and clumsy.

She'd thrown a potion of slowness at me, the witch.

"Well, if I can't have a wither servant, I can at least get myself a nether star. You're useful to me dead or alive, and you've made it clear that I'm not going to get you alive."

She pulled out another potion, but I wasn't going to let her hit me with it. Summoning all my strength, I sent a blue skull in her direction, the force of my throw pushing me backwards down the stairs to her hut.

"Noooo!" cried Mabel as her hut erupted in a ball of flame. She rushed in to try and save her belongings from the fire and I took the opportunity to slither away.

It took a while for the potion to wear off, but luckily the witch was too distracted to try and stop me escaping and soon I was far away from her evil clutches.

Lesson learned. Don't trust witches unless they're your mom.

Day 10

I found something very strange as I was making my way through the woods. It was a door, but it didn't have a building, so it was just standing in the middle of a clearing all by itself leading nowhere. Inside the frame, instead of a wooden or metal door, was purple sparkles and as I drew closer, a strange noise came from it, a kind of humming, but nothing like anything I'd heard before.

I walked all around. You couldn't see through the purple sparkles, and they pulsated and glowed on either side.

Curioser and curioser.

I decided to touch the purple sparkles to see if they were solid. Carefully, I moved forward. The moment my head touched the sparkles, WHOOSH!

Everything went black.

Day 11

My eyes fluttered open. Everything was dark around me. Had I slept until night time?

I sat up and looked around. It was dark because I was underground. Torches lit up the space I was in and strange moans and groans filtered through the air. If I didn't know that I was incredibly powerful, I would be very frightened. As it was, I was still feeling uneasy at finding myself in such a strange place.

I looked above me, expecting to see a hole in the ground that I'd fallen through. Nothing. Just a dark ceiling.

I stood up. Behind me was an exact replica of the strange doorway I'd seen in the forest.

Was this some kind of portal to a nether world?

"I wonder…" I stepped forward. Taking a deep breath, I moved into the purple sparkles.

WHOOSH! I was back in the forest!

I stepped through the doorway.

WHOOSH! I was back in the nether world!

I don't know how long I spent stepping back and forth through the door, switching between the two worlds. It was so much fun!

"What are you doing?"

When I stepped out into the Nether, a skeleton was standing in front of the door. "Anyone would think you'd never seen a Nether portal before."

"I haven't," I replied. "And I haven't seen a talking skeleton either."

"Wow. You've led a sheltered life. Where have you been – in a swamp somewhere?"

"Why, yes! How did you guess?"

The skeleton whistled through its teeth, making a strange, rattling noise. I had no idea that skeletons could whistle. "I was just being silly. I didn't think withers liked getting their tails wet."

"I don't," I admitted. "But that's where my mom lives."

"Your mom? There's a wither that likes living in the swamp?"

"My mom's not a wither. She's a witch."

The skeleton's jaw dropped to the floor and he had to fumble about to fix it back again. When his jaw was back in place, he was a little more careful about showing how shocked he was. "Your mom's a witch? How could that happen?"

I told him the story my mom had told me, about how she'd created me to help her. "And now she's sent me out into the world to find other withers," I finished. "It was really sweet of her. I know how much she's going to miss me."

"Sweet?" The skeleton snickered. "You really are dumb! Witches aren't sweet. They don't do anything nice for anyone. The only person they care about is themselves."

"That's not true!" I protested. "My mom cares about me."

"Really? So I suppose you had your own bedroom and lots of toys to play with growing up?"

"Not exactly…" I thought about the basket at the foot of mom's bed where I used to sleep curled up on a cushion. I always thought it was really kind of her to let me sleep inside, but maybe mom could have done more for me. "But what kind of toys do withers play with anyway?"

"Oh, I don't know," the skeleton shrugged. "I don't really care. I'm just saying that if your mom has sent you out to find other withers, I don't think it's because she cares so much about you. Perhaps she's got some kind of plan for those withers."

"You're wrong! She does care!"

"Suit yourself. No skin off my nose." The skeleton giggled. "See what I did there? No skin off my nose." He walked off, still laughing at his silly joke.

Day 12

I couldn't sleep last night. Maybe I should have gone back to the forest to get some peace from the strange noises in the Nether, but it probably wouldn't have made any difference. I was too worried thinking about what the skeleton had said.

Mom had been the only person I'd known all my life. She had to care about me. She'd been looking after me all this time, hadn't she?

And yet what the skeleton said had made sense. Mom had talked about me bringing back some withers to meet her. Was that really because she wanted to meet my friends or did she have some other reason behind needing me to take some withers to meet her? If I was powerful on my own, imagine how powerful a whole horde of withers could be!

Maybe she was trying to raise a wither army to take over the world!

I couldn't help but laugh at the idea. If that's what mom wanted to do, all she had to do was ask. She knew that I'd do anything to help her.

That was probably it. Mom just needed my help, but didn't feel like she could ask me outright. Silly mom. She should know that I'd do anything for her. She is my mom, after all!

Day 13

Now that I've been in the Nether for a couple of days, I'm starting to really feel at home here. I found a settlement today. After my experiences with the villagers, I was worried about going too close, but as I drew near, nobody came out to attack me. In fact, everyone just ignored me as they went about their business.

"Excuse me," I asked a passing creature. "What is this place?"

"Grooooaaaannnn!"

"I'm sorry, I didn't quite understand. Could you repeat that please?"

"GROOOOAAAANNNN!"

"You should know better than to try and talk to a zombie!" giggled a passing skeleton. "They only have half a brain at the best of times!"

"Then maybe you could help me. I was wondering what this place was called?"

"This is Herobrine's Haven," replied the skeleton. "A fortress full of Nether creatures and creatures who hate humans."

I gulped. Mom was human. If everyone in the fortress hated humans, would they hate me because I'd been raised by one?

The skeleton left before I could ask him any more questions, but now I wasn't sure what to do. Should I go into the fortress and try to blend in? Or should I go back to the portal and continue my search in Minecraftia?

I decided to go and find somewhere to camp for the night. I could decide what to do in the morning.

Day 14

I woke up feeling determined. I made my way over to the Nether fortress.

I was going to go into Herobrine's Haven and see if I could find anyone who'd seen a wither. They seemed a lot friendlier down here and nobody needed to know that mom was a witch – as long as the skeleton I'd spoken to the other day hadn't told anyone.

Maybe I should track him down and smash his bones to smithereens!

The thought was gone as soon as I had it, but I couldn't believe that I'd even had the idea in the first place. My true wither nature must be showing through. Mabel had told me that withers usually attacked just about anyone they met, which was how she'd known I was different from the moment she first saw me. I guess that's why she had tried to get me to stay with her.

"Hey, you! Move out the way! You're blocking the entrance to the fortress!"

An angry skeleton shoved me out of the way. I'd been so lost in thought that I hadn't realized that people were trying to get past.

Unprepared, I stumbled, teetering on the edge of the bridge that led into the fortress. I tried to get my balance back, but it was no good. I fell into the lava stream flowing around the building.

"Aargh!" I screamed. "I'm burning. Somebody save me!"

"Stop being so stupid!" yelled a voice from the bridge. "You're not burning or drowning. Just climb up the steps!"

I stopped flailing around. They were right! I wasn't burning! In fact, the molten rock felt rather pleasant flowing all over me, making me feel all warm and tingly as if I were snuggled up in a cozy blanket.

I lay back in the lava, happy to simply float there. I hadn't felt this peaceful since I'd left the swamp. I could just spend all day here.

I closed my eyes, drifting away as the lava moat carried me around the outside of the Nether fortress.

"Incoming!"

My blissful reverie was shattered by the sound of a guard calling for reinforcements. For a moment, I ducked under the lava as I struggled to get to the side, but I soon found my balance. I pulled myself out of the moat and hurried back to the bridge leading to Herobrine's Haven.

Two Minecraftians were firing arrows at the guards on the battlements as a horde of zombies lurched towards them. It was clear that they'd attacked first and all the Nether creatures were being called to help fight them off.

I charged towards the Minecraftians, skulls shooting from me.

"Withers!" cried one of the Minecraftians.

"Run!" yelled the other.

They turned and raced away. I could have chased after them, but the pack of zombie pigmen racing after them were likely to finish the job.

Besides, I was more intrigued by the fact that they hadn't talked about just one wither – they'd been afraid of withers.

I turned around, desperately trying to spot the other withers, but I couldn't see any. Maybe I'd heard them wrong.

As much as I was disappointed not to have found other withers, I couldn't help but feel proud of the fact that I'd been able to scare the humans so easily all by myself.

Day 15

I wasn't wrong! There was another wither in the fortress! The reason I hadn't seen them was because they were just coming out of the door to see what all the noise was about, and they'd gone back into the fortress as soon as they realized the humans were leaving before I'd had a chance to see them.

After the fight, I felt brave enough to go into the fortress. After all, I'd gone into battle shoulder to shoulder with these guys. If that didn't make me one of them, I don't know what would.

The inside of the fortress was amazing. It was absolutely huge! I'd never seen a building so big. Everywhere I looked, Nether creatures dashed about doing whatever it was skeletons and zombies did. Nobody paid any attention to me as I made my way through the courtyard, gazing about in wonder. Stairs led up to the battlements, and doors led into the depths of the fortress. There were so many choices, I didn't know where to go first.

"Are you lost, little one?"

I turned and there he was. The other wither.

"You're real!" I gasped. "You're really real! I'm not alone!"

"Of course you're not alone," chuckled the wither. "What on earth made you think you would be the only wither on the planet?"

"Er… the fact that I've never met another wither?" I mumbled.

"I've never met the Ender dragon, but I know it exists," pointed out the wither.

"He does?! I thought that was just a story witches told their children to get them to behave when they're being naughty."

"Are you serious?" The wither laughed again. "You are the strangest wither I've ever met."

"You mean you've met other withers?"

"Of course I have, silly. Heck, there's one of them staying in the fortress right now."

"Really?"

"Really. Would you like to go and meet him?"

"I'd love to!"

The wither led me through a door at the back of the courtyard, down twisted corridors and into a large room.

"Hey, Jerry! I've just met the funniest wither! You've got to say hello!"

I wasn't sure how I felt about being described as 'funny', but I slithered forward to say hello. "Hi Jerry. I'm Willis."

"Oh, I'm so sorry," said the first wither. "I forgot to introduce myself. I'm Henry."

"Hi, Henry."

"So tell Jerry what you were saying to me," Henry told me.

"Well, it's just that I've never met another wither before. I thought I was the only one in Minecraftia. In fact, it was only recently that I discovered that I'm a wither and not-"

"Not what?"

I could have kicked myself. How could I have been so stupid? I'd told myself to pretend I was just a normal wither and not the son of a witch and I'd almost blurted it out in my excitement at having met other withers like me.

"Oh, not a zombie," I finished weakly, unable to quickly think of a better reply.

"A zombie?" Jerry and Henry laughed.

"You're right, Henry. This guy's hilarious!"

Day 16

I've been having the best time with Jerry and Henry. They've taken me all over the fortress and introduced me to everyone who lives there. It's so good to be among friends. Withers are really popular down here because we're so strong. No wonder those Minecraftians ran away as soon as they saw us.

"What's that up there?"

I pointed to a strange light glowing at the top of a tower.

Jerry and Henry exchanged a sad look.

"That's Brian," Jerry replied.

"Brian?" I frowned. "What do you mean? Is the beacon a person or something?"

"Something," Jerry told me. "You see, when a wither is killed, we drop a very precious item called a nether star. Nether stars can be used to create beacons like the one up there."

"You mean-?"

"That's right," nodded Henry sadly. "That's all that remains of our good friend, Brian, a fellow wither. He was killed in battle, but before the evil Minecraftian who slew him could take the nether star, we got him. We decided that the best tribute to Brian would be for us to make a beacon in his name. As long as it shines, all the inhabitants of the fortress are stronger and our morale is high. Brian will always be with us in spirit."

I looked up at the beacon, tears misting over my eyes. I had no idea that withers were so powerful even after death. No wonder mom took so long to tell me what I really was. She must have been trying to keep me safe from all the Minecraftians who would try to kill me for a nether star.

Day 17

Jerry and Henry have been taking me all over the Nether. I had no idea that this was such a cool place! There are so many friendly people here. Even the zombie pigmen are friendly once you get the hang of understanding their grunts and groans.

They taught me how to play witherball. It's sooo much fun! It's better the more withers you have to play with, so we teamed up with a few other withers who were in the area and spent the afternoon playing.

You divide yourselves into two teams and you each have a goal on four sides of the pitch. You win points by either blowing up your opponents' goal or throwing a skull through their goal. If the other team blows up your goal, you can rebuild it, but that can leave your other goals open to attack.

Billy the Blaze was the referee, and it was good that he was there – witherball can get really rough! One of the other withers ran into me just as I was about to throw a skull at their goal. My skull veered off to one side and narrowly missed my own goal. I'm glad it didn't hit – that would have cost my team five points. As it was, it blew a huge hole in the wall and angry skeleton archers fired arrows back at us, yelling at us to be more careful.

"Did you enjoy that?" asked Jerry as the final whistle blew.

"It was great! I want to play again," I replied. "Maybe next time our team will win!"

"It was close," nodded Henry. "If that final skull they shot hadn't caught the edge of our goal, blowing it up while the force of the blast tossed the skull through, we would have won. It was a brilliant play – I just wished that wither had been on our team!"

"Every year, we hold a big witherball tournament just outside of Herobrine's Haven," Jerry told me. "You should come. You're a natural defender. I'd love to have you on my team."

"I'd like that," I blushed. A huge tournament! Withers from all over the world! I could hardly wait to meet them all.

Day 18

"Do you really think I'm good enough to play in the witherball tournament, Henry?" I asked him eagerly. "After all, I've only just started playing."

"You have," nodded Henry, "but you're a natural! I mean, look at the way you scored that goal this morning."

I couldn't help but beam as I remembered the goal I'd scored when I'd sent a skull in the direction of a goal, missing, but watching it bounce off the wall and through one of the other goals. "It was a lucky shot, but it was pretty awesome, wasn't it?"

"You seem to have a lot of lucky shots," Henry observed. "I'd love to have you on my team. Besides, the witherball tournament is for everyone, even withers who've only just started playing. It's just as much about having fun as it is being the best at witherball."

"Then I'd love to be on your team," I grinned. My smile faded as a thought occurred to me. "I just wish that mom could be there to see it."

"She can," Henry replied. "After all, we need people to cheer us on, don't we? And plenty of zombies come along to watch. It's the highlight of the Nether calendar."

"Oh yes. Zombies." I'd forgotten that I'd told Henry that mom was a zombie.

I decided the time had come to take a chance. I was going to tell Henry the truth.

"Listen, Henry. There's something I need to tell you about my mom."

"What is it?"

I was just about to tell him when Jerry came rushing up. "Hey, guys! A couple of Minecraftians have been firing arrows at the blazes. There's a big fight brewing and it looks like a lot of fun."

"A fight?" Henry and I looked at each other. "Let's go!"

Day 19

I really want to tell Henry the truth about mom. Out of all the withers I've met since coming to the nether, I think he's the one who would understand. He seems so kind and lovely.

The problem is that every time I get close to telling him, something happens to stop me. Yesterday it was the fight with the Minecraftians. Today it was a game of witherball that started without warning. If I'm going to compete in the tournament, I need all the practice I can get, so I had to join. After the game, Henry went off with Jerry, so I didn't get a chance to talk to him.

I don't know what to do.

Day 20

Today I finally got a chance to talk to Henry. We were walking down by the lava lake and no one was around to hear what I had to say. I knew that if I didn't tell him the truth about mom, I'd never get a better chance, and I hated the thought of lying to someone who's been such a good friend to me.

"Henry," I began. "Do you remember me telling you that my mom is a zombie?"

"Yes," replied Henry. "I still can't understand that. It's so weird! Usually zombies don't do anything but grunt and groan and look for brains. It's really strange that one of them was able to bring up a wither, especially one as cool as you."

I blushed. "Thanks, Henry, that's really kind of you to say. It makes what I've got to tell you even harder."

"What do you mean?"

"I think you'd better sit down."

Henry sat down, a worried look on his face. "What's wrong, Willis?"

"It's my mom. She's not a zombie."

Henry looked up at me, his expression impossible to read.

I took a deep breath. "She's a witch."

Henry nodded slowly. "That explains a lot."

"What do you mean?"

"Well, there are certain little things about the way you talk that reminded me of witches, and I never could quite believe your story about a zombie. Your mom being a witch makes a lot more sense."

"So you're not mad at me for lying to you?"

"Not at all. Humans aren't exactly popular around here, even if they're witches. I don't blame you for wanting to keep it quiet. In fact, if I were you, I wouldn't tell anyone else, not even Jerry. The other withers might not be as understanding as me."

"OK. If you think that's the best thing to do."

"I'm just thinking of you."

"Thanks, Henry." I had an idea. "Listen. If mom disguised herself as a zombie, do you think she could come and watch me play in the witherball tournament?"

Henry whistled. "Wow, Willis. You really like to make things difficult for yourself, don't you?!"

"It's just that I know that mom would be so proud of me if she could see me with all the other withers, and I know that she'll be worrying about me out here by myself. When she's watched the tournament, she'll see that everything is OK and I've found my true family."

"I'm not sure." Henry looked thoughtful. "Tell you what. Why don't I come back with you to see your mom? She sounds like an interesting character. I'd like to meet her, and if I think that we can smuggle her in to the tournament, then I'll do everything I can to keep her safe."

"Will you?" I could have hugged Henry. "Then let's go back to the swamp! I can't wait for you to meet my mom."

Day 21

Henry and I didn't leave yesterday after a heated game of witherball happened. I love playing that game!

Henry was one of the team captains. He put me on defending the goal and I managed to deflect not just one, not two, but three skulls! Our team won by three points, so I made all the difference between us winning and losing.

"See, Willis?" Henry said to me. "I told you that you were a natural at this game. You need to be here for the tournament."

"I will," I promised. "But I'd love it if mom was here too."

"All right. Let's go and see if we can talk her into coming to the nether to support her boy."

"You mean it?"

"Of course! I told you I was going to come with you. Why not go now?"

Why not exactly?

Henry and I said goodbye to the other withers, promising that we'd be back in time for the tournament before heading off to the nearest nether portal.

I was going home to mom and I was bringing another wither with me!

Day 22

Henry and I left the Nether through a different portal than the one I'd arrived by, so it took me a while to get my bearings.

At last, I was able to figure out the right direction to go in by seeing where the sun was setting. "We need to go that way," I told Henry firmly, hoping that he wouldn't notice my disorientation as I pointed towards some trees in the distance.

"Are you sure?" Henry asked. "You don't seem very sure."

"Of course I'm sure!" I replied. "This is where I grew up. Of course I know where it is."

We started walking and Henry told me stories about his childhood.

"I was made by a Minecraftian living in the desert. I think he had an idea that he was going to get a nether star by killing me, but there was no way I was going to let that happen. I left him for dust and disappeared off into the heart of the desert where I met up with some other withers. We traveled around Minecraftia together for a while until I decided that I wanted to go down and see what it was like in the Nether. I fell in love with the place, and it's been my home ever since. It's been ages since I've been up here. It hasn't changed much."

I couldn't imagine what it must be like being created just so that someone could kill you and get a nether star.

There are some terrible people in this world.

Day 23

As we went over the top of a hill, a village sat quietly in the valley below.

"Look at that," Henry said to me. "All those people peacefully going about their business. They have no idea that two withers are about to come down on them like a ton of bricks!"

"What, you mean that we should attack them?"

"Of course!" Henry laughed. "I'm sorry, Willis. Sometimes I forget that you were raised by a witch. You seem so normal most of the time."

"Thanks, Henry!" I laughed with him.

"Do you really mean to say that you don't have a really strong urge to run down there and blow up all their buildings?" Henry asked.

I looked down at the buildings below. "To be honest, I'd love to see what it would be like if all those houses were on fire."

"Well what are we waiting for? Those buildings aren't going to destroy themselves!"

Henry started racing down the hill and I followed close on his heels, skulls shooting out in all directions.

BOOM! I scored a direct hit on a building, sending villagers screaming and running in all directions.

"You're right, Henry. This is fun!" I laughed as we made our way through the town, causing chaos wherever we went.

The iron golems came out to defend the village, but they were too late. The damage was already done. The whole village was on fire and Henry and I ran away, giggling like schoolboys, leaving the villagers behind to try and rebuild their homes.

"This is what life as a wither is supposed to be like!" Henry shouted at me as we raced off as far away from the village as we could. Withers are powerful, but we're not immortal. If we'd stayed around for too long, we'd have given them a chance to get their defenses together and fight us off.

As it was, the village was going to take a long time to rebuild and I couldn't help but laugh as I thought about how hard they were going to have to work to put together new homes and workplaces for all the villagers.

We headed into the forest on the other side of the village. "I think I know where we are," I told Henry. "If I'm right, there should be some plains past the forest and then the swamp after that. We're not far from my home now."

"Cool! I can't wait to meet your mom. Do you think she's going to like me?"

"Of course she will!" I assured Henry. "Why wouldn't she? You're the best wither I've ever met."

"Until recently, I was just about the only wither you'd ever met," Henry reminded me.

"That's true, but that doesn't change the fact that you're still a great wither, and someone I'm really proud to know," I told him.

"And that's why you're such a nice guy!" replied Henry. "You always see the best in people. I'm sure your mom is just as nice as you are, and I can't wait to meet her so I can tell her what a great job she's done bringing you up."

I blushed with pride as I thought about how lucky I am. I could never have dreamed that I was going to meet someone like Henry when mom sent me off into the world to find more of my kind. Now I was taking him back to my mom, and together we were going to come up with a way of smuggling mom down to the Nether and keeping her safe so she could watch me compete in the witherball tournament.

I love my life!

Day 24

"There it is! The swamp! That's my home!" I couldn't contain my excitement as I led Henry in the direction of the swamp. It felt like I'd been away forever.

Henry held his nose as we drew closer. "It stinks! How could you have put up with the smell all those years?"

I shrugged. "It's not so bad after a while. You get used to it. Come on. Mom's hut is this way. She'll be so pleased to see us. I can't wait for you to meet her!"

I rushed forward, pointing out all my favorite places to Henry. "There's the log where I like to sit and watch the birds flying. There's the lake where you can get lots of fish. There's the remains of the hut that belonged to the witch who used to live here before mom moved in."

I'd enjoyed exploring Minecraftia, but there was no place like home. It felt good to be back.

At last, we reached mom's hut. "Mom? Are you in here?" I went up the steps to the hut and peeked through the door. It was empty.

"She must be out gathering ingredients," I said to Henry. "Come in and I'll make us some food."

Henry followed me up the stairs to mom's hut. It was very cramped inside with two withers together. I'd forgotten how small it was. Maybe now that I'd seen Herobrine's Haven, I could talk mom into extending it a bit. She deserved her own bedroom at least, and there was plenty of space for a bigger hut.

There wasn't much food in the cupboards, but I managed to find enough to create a tasty rabbit stew. "Sorry that's all there is," I apologized, as I put a bowl down in front of Henry.

He took a spoonful. "Don't apologize. This tastes amazing!"

We stayed up talking until late at night, but there was no sign of mom. "She must be off on one of her ingredient gathering missions," I said to Henry. "Not to worry. She'll be back soon. Meanwhile, why don't you sleep on the bed and I'll curl up in my basket?"

"Your basket?"

"Oh yes." I slithered over to the corner of the room where my basket and its comfortable cushion were still sitting. "I love my basket!"

"Are you sure you wouldn't rather have a bed? I'm surprised your mom didn't make space for one. It wouldn't take much, and you'd have room to stretch out."

"No, no, I'm fine," I assured him, although now that he'd said it, I did wonder why mom had never given me a bed.

I decided to ask her about it when she got back.

Day 25

When I woke up the next morning, for a moment, I wasn't sure where I was. Then I remembered. I was back home!

I yawned and stretched. "Did you sleep all right, Henry?"

No reply.

I looked over at the bed. It was empty. "Henry? Where are you, Henry?"

Still no reply.

I went outside. "Mom! It's so good to see you again!"

Mom jumped as I raced over to her to give her a big hug. "Oh. Willis. I wasn't expecting to see you just yet."

"Yeah, well, I had a lot of fun exploring the world but I was missing you and anyway, I had a friend I wanted you to meet, only I don't know where he is. He was sleeping in your bed – I hope you don't mind."

"Of course I don't mind," mom assured me. "A friend of yours is a friend of mine. He was more than welcome to use my bed while I was away. But I'm sorry to say that I haven't seen any withers around the swamp this morning. I guess he must have gone. You know what withers are like. They can be very unreliable."

"Really?" A frown wrinkled my forehead. "Henry didn't seem like he was unreliable."

"Appearances can be deceptive," mom reminded me. "People aren't always what they seem. If I were you, I'd go and check the cupboards, make sure he didn't steal anything."

"Henry wouldn't!" Would he?

Mom just looked at me.

I hurried inside, frantically opening cupboards and checking to make sure that everything was where mom had left it. As far as I could see, everything was where it should be.

"Nothing's gone, mom," I said as I went back outside, but she was gone.

This was all very strange. People were disappearing all over the place!

Day 26

Mom has been acting very strangely. When I told her about the witherball tournament, she didn't seem as excited about it as I thought she would be. Maybe it was the idea of dressing up as a zombie or maybe she doesn't really like sports, but every time I try to bring it up, she changes the subject or finds things for me to do in the witch hut and then goes off into the swamp without me.

When I asked her what she was doing, she said that she was just looking for more mushrooms, but that's even stranger. We have loads of mushrooms already. She doesn't need any more.

At last I decided to follow her to see what she was up to. There was a bit of me that didn't want to. If mom was keeping something secret, it would be for a good reason. Maybe she was planning a big surprise birthday party!

I waited until she'd gone into the swamp before following her from a distance. Luckily, withers are really good at tracking, and I could see where she'd gone from the ripples in the swamp water and broken twigs where she'd brushed past bushes. I didn't need to keep her in sight to know where she'd gone.

At last, mom came to a stop in a clearing. She was standing in front of a strange box that I'd never seen before. Frowning, I slithered forward to get a closer look, snapping a branch as I moved.

Mom looked over and I quickly ducked down so that she wouldn't see me. Something told me that I didn't want her to know that I was watching.

At last, she turned her attention back to the box and I peeped over the log I was crouching behind. "Not long now, my pretty," I heard her say to whatever was inside. "You have no idea how long it's taken me to get something like you. I've tried to make so many withers since Willis and I don't know what I'm doing wrong, but he's been my only success. When you need a lot of nether stars, you're hardly going to kill your only wither are you?"

I gasped, ducking down again, hoping that she hadn't heard me. She was too caught up in her ramblings to listen and besides, she thought that I was busy sorting out the wood for the fire.

"No, I soon realized that if I wanted to build the most powerful beacon Minecraftia has ever seen, I was going to have to send a wither to catch a wither, so I sent Willis out in the world, knowing that the silly thing would soon bring back all the withers I need. One isn't much, but it's a start and now that he's found you, others are sure to follow.

I know you've been trying to escape, but there are special enchantments on that box, and you're not going anywhere until I've got a few more of your friends. Then I'll be able to harvest all the nether stars I want and no one will be able to stop me."

Henry! Henry was in the box and mom was going to kill him!

I could have kicked myself for being so stupid. All the withers had told me that you couldn't trust a human, but I thought that she cared about me. All along, mom had just been using me to get what she wanted.

Well, she wasn't going to succeed. If she thought that she had a good plan, it was nothing compared to what a wither could do when we put our minds to it.

Day 27

Mom stayed out really late, so I pretended to be asleep when she got back. I waited until she was snoring before swallowing a potion of invisibility. Moving my cushions about so that it looked like I was still curled up in my basket, I slithered out and off in the direction of the box she was keeping Henry in.

As I stood in front of the box, it glowed eerily in the moonlight, the enchantment making the walls pulsate almost as though they were alive. "Henry? Are you in there?"

"Willis? Is that you?"

A dark shape unfurled from a corner of the box and slithered forward, hovering in front of the small hole she'd left as a window.

"Oh my goodness, Henry. Look what she's done to you. I am so sorry! I would never have brought you back here if I knew that this was what mom had planned."

"Don't worry, Willis. All us withers know that you can't trust humans. That's why we attack them as soon as we see them – so they don't get us first. But you were brought up by her. She made sure that you couldn't know how wicked humans really are. It's not your fault."

"Well, I'm going to make up for it. I'm going to get you out of here."

"Thanks, Willis."

I looked around for a bolt on the door, but I couldn't see anything that looked like a door, let alone a way to open it. I picked up a stick and hit the wall with it, but as soon as the stick touched the box, it disintegrated!

"All right, Henry. Stand back. I'm going to throw a skull at the box."

"Willis, don't-"

Summoning all my strength, I hurled three skulls at the box.

BOOM!

The jungle shuddered, birds flew from the trees screaming in protest, but when the dust settled, the box was still in the middle of the clearing, completely untouched.

"I tried to warn you," Henry said. "I already tried that. The witch has put an enchantment on the box so our attacks don't work on it."

"How are we going to open it then?" I could have cried in despair. "I can't leave you here."

"The witch said something when she threw me in here. I think there's a little spell that opens it up."

My heart sank. If there was an incantation that opened the box, we didn't have a hope.

"Sorry, Henry. You're going to have to stay here for a bit longer while I figure this out. But don't worry. I'm going to rescue you, one way or another. I promise."

The sun was rising over the horizon and I knew that mom was going to wake up soon. I didn't want her to know that I'd tried to get Henry out of the box. "I better go now, but I'll be back for you. Just sit tight."

Poor Henry. He didn't really have much of a choice but to stay where he was. I just hoped that I could solve the mystery of the box before it was too late.

Day 28

"What's wrong, Willis?"

I jumped as mom sneaked up behind me. I thought she was still out at the box and I was looking through the cabinets to see if I could find something that would help me free Henry.

"I was just looking for some glistering melon, mom," I replied, thinking quickly. "I thought I'd make some more health potions. I noticed that our stocks were getting low."

"That's my Willis. Always such a good boy." Mom smiled warmly and ruffled the top of my head.

Phew! It looked as though I'd gotten away with it, but I was going to have to be careful if I was going to find a way of releasing Henry and I was running out of time.

Day 29

I'd turned the witch hut upside down and still hadn't found anything that might give me a clue to opening the box. I'd lost a whole day searching and wasn't any closer to helping Henry. I lay in my basket, tossing and turning as I desperately tried to think of what I could do to save my friend.

"Oh Willis."

I jumped, thinking that mom was talking to me, but when I looked over at her bed, she rolled over and snorted. She was talking in her sleep.

She does that sometimes.

Wait a minute – she talks in her sleep! When I was younger, I used to make myself laugh by talking to her and having whole conversations that she couldn't remember in the morning. Maybe this was the opportunity I needed.

"Mom, what colour are your socks?" I whispered softly, not wanting to wake her up, but needing to see if she really was sleep talking.

"Red and white," she muttered.

"What's your favorite food?"

"Pumpkin pie."

"How do you get into the wither box?"

"Walk round it three times, chanting wither in, wither out and then throw some glowstone dust over it."

Oh my goodness! I almost squealed with excitement! I could set Henry free!

Carefully, I tiptoed over to the cupboard where we kept our glowstone dust. Luckily, we still had plenty and I grabbed a handful before drinking another potion of invisibility to go out to the box.

Normally, I'd take my time to admire the way the moonlight glittered on the swamp water, but I was a wither on a mission and I had a friend to save.

When I reached the box, I called to Henry. "Henry! Henry! Are you in there?"

Silence. Was I too late?

"Willis? Is that you?" A sleepy voice came from the depths of the box. He'd just been asleep. Thank goodness!

"Yes, it's me and I know how to get you out of the box."

"Hurry, Willis. The witch told me she was going to get her first nether star today. We don't have much time."

I started walking round the box. "Wither in, wither out, wither in, wither out."

Henry started chanting with me, our voices coming together as the air started to shimmer from the effect of the magic spell. "Wither in, wither out, wither in, wither out."

I grabbed some glowstone dust. "Wither in, wither OUT!"

With the final word, I threw the dust over the box.

BOOM!

The sides of the box fell away, the top flying off to goodness knows where. Henry was free!

"Run, Henry! You have to get as far away as you can!"

"But what about you, Willis? You have to come with me."

"No." I shook my head. "I need to talk to mom. I need her to know that she can't mess with withers. I'll join you later at Herobrine's Haven. Now go. Mom is going to wake up soon and we don't have much time."

Henry looked as though he was going to argue, but he didn't say anything, turning and slithering off to disappear into the depths of the swamp.

Day 30

"Nooooooooooooooooooooooooooooooo!"

Mom's scream of frustration was so loud that it echoed throughout the swamp. I couldn't help but grin. She must have just discovered that Henry was gone.

"Oh dear, mom," I said to myself. "Don't you have any withers to kill? What a shame!"

"Willis! Where are you, Willis?"

I could hear her crashing and bashing her way through the forest as she came to find me. A little nervous knot tied itself in my stomach as I went out of the witch's hut to meet her.

"I'm right here, mom," I called as she came storming up the path to the hut.

Before I could say anything more, she pulled out a splash potion of slowness, throwing it straight in my face.

"You stay right there, young man!"

I restrained the urge to throw a skull at her. Even though she'd tried to hurt my friend, she was still my mom. She wouldn't do anything to hurt me.

"What happened to my box?" she demanded.

I shrugged, unable to keep the smug grin off my face.

"What. Happened. To. My. Box?" She pulled out another potion and I paled when I realized that she had a potion of poison in her hand.

Maybe she would do something to hurt me.

"You told me how to open it," I replied.

"No I didn't. I wouldn't!"

"Yes, you did. You were talking in your sleep, so I decided to see if you'd tell me how to free Henry. You gave me the chant and I let him go."

"Why would you do such a thing, you wicked boy?! Now my years of planning are all for nothing. You've ruined everything!"

She pulled back her arm to throw the potion at me. "Well, if I can't get all the withers I need, I'll just have to make do with this one."

"Oh no you don't."

The witch whirled round and I could have cheered at what I saw. Henry was back and he wasn't alone! Hundreds of withers crowded into the clearing where we lived.

"You hurt one hair on Willis' head and we'll make you wish he'd never been born. Now let him go."

For a moment, I thought that mom was mad enough to take on the horde of withers, but she wasn't that stupid and she stepped past to let me join my friends.

"What do you want us to do with her?" asked Henry.

"Let's blast her and her hut to smithereens!" cried one of the withers.

"Yes! Yes! Destroy her! Destroy the witch!"

All the withers started to press forward as mom cowered at the entrance to her hut.

"NO!"

My shout was so forceful, everyone fell silent immediately. "I know she did a terrible thing, but she's still my mom. Let her live – for now."

I turned to the witch I'd thought of as my mom for so long. "But let it be known that if I ever hear that you've tried to collect nether stars again, we will return and make sure that the entire swamp is destroyed. There will be nothing left of you or your home by the time we've finished with you."

"Don't worry," mom promised. "I'm not going to have anything to do with withers ever again. You're far too much trouble."

"Good." I turned to my fellow withers. "Come on, everyone. We've got a witherball tournament to get to. The witch will leave us alone now."

The withers cheered and turned to leave the swamp. "How did you get back so quickly?" I asked Henry.

"I made a nether portal not far from here and went for reinforcements. I had a funny feeling that the witch wasn't going to be very happy with you, so I brought back a few friends to make sure you were safe."

"Thanks, Henry. You're the best."

As we reached the portal to the Nether, I thought about how lucky I was. I might have been created by a witch, but I was a wither and proud of it.

"OK, Willis," said Henry as withers started pouring through the portal. "Let's go play some witherball! We've got a tournament to win."

I followed him through the portal, happy to have found my real family at last.

Made in the USA
Columbia, SC
14 December 2019